Joanne B. Parrotta

The Little Gold Book of
Money and Happiness

A Guide to Your Financial Success

WiseAdviceBooks

Inspiring to Become Healthy, Wealthy and Wise!

Table of Contents

*I dedicate this little book to my readers. By picking up **The Little Gold Book of Money and Happiness** you have taken the first step towards financial freedom.*

Congratulations!

"Before everything else, getting ready is the secret of success."
—Henry Ford

Introduction

Just imagine that you had enough money to do what you wanted when you wanted. Imagine a life in which you had no more financial worries, a life in which you could travel whenever you wanted, wherever you wanted. How about a life in which you could retire comfortably, at whatever age you choose?

Sound impossible?

Would it surprise you to know that there are millions of people in this country doing just that? They are the financially free. How do they do it? What is their secret? What do they know that you don't?

Before I begin to answer these and many other questions, let me say that if you're looking for easy wealth and get-rich-quick schemes, you have picked up the wrong book. But if you are looking for tools, ideas, and inspiration, you've come to the right place. In this little book I will not be telling you how to invest your money. Although I do offer some suggestions, that topic is beyond my scope of expertise. An overwhelming amount of information is available on creating wealth (including

1

advice on topics such as personal finance, small businesses, entrepreneurship, trading, and investing) and countless financial advisers would be more than happy to help you invest your money. In this book I hope to provide you with the inspiration, tools, and skills you need to start your journey to a life free of financial worries. Ready to get started? Your adventure begins now.

To your success!
Joanne B. Parrotta

Chapter 1 * Making the Dream a Reality

Money is neither my god nor my devil. It is a form of energy that tends to make us more of who we already are, whether it's greedy or loving.
— *Dan Millman*

Wealth is not something that happens only to others. It can happen to you. You, too, can be rich. Now, I don't mean super-rich (unless that's what you really want). You don't have to be another Donald Trump, and you don't have to win the lottery or wait for a relative to pass away and leave you tons of money. You can do it all yourself. To get started just follow the simple steps outlined in this book.

Let's face it, *money matters*. While money is not everything, it is important. People who say otherwise are just fooling themselves. Without money we cannot be totally free. We cannot send our children to college. We

3

cannot retire comfortably. We cannot live the life of which we've always dreamed.

I completely agree that there are more important things in life than money. No amount of money in the world can buy us good health or a great spouse and children, nor can it buy us true friends or a job that we love. In fact, money alone, without all these other wonderful things, will never make us truly happy. But if you play your cards right, you can have these things and lots of money, too. Keep in mind, though, that hoarding or obsessing about money can rob you of the richness of life. As with all things, there must be balance.

Now, before you take the first step towards financial freedom, you must acknowledge that your financial life is not where you want it to be and that you are looking to change it. You must truly believe in your heart that you will do whatever it takes to change your financial situation for the better. Don't feel bad or put yourself down for being where you are. The fact that you are holding this book is significant—it shows that you have taken control. Congratulations!

Now you can tend to the business of setting your goals and following the advice in this (and other) books, and the money will follow.

Issues Surrounding Money

"Whatever the mind of man can conceive and believe, it can achieve"

— *Napoleon Hill, author of* Think and Grow Rich

Many people in our society have serious issues surrounding money. If this is true of you, they must be dealt with before you can go on. The first step towards financial freedom is to know where your attitudes about money come from and what your money personality is.

Ask yourself the following questions:

- What does money mean to me and what are my attitudes about money?
- What did my parents teach me about money?

Think back to your childhood, because that is when your relationship with money started. Try to remember some of the events that may have shaped your attitudes about money. Our subconscious mind remembers everything.

Our parents, relatives, friends, and teachers have all contributed to our beliefs about money. Old thoughts continue to influence our lives, and for many of us the answer to the first question above lies in the past. If you have negative attitudes about money, knowing where they come from will help you take control of your money. You will gain enormous insight into your past and how your financial habits evolved.

Remember that everything you have been through in your life has shaped who you are today, so please do not blame your parents (or others) if you think they might have contributed in a negative way to your financial situation. They could not possibly have taught you anything they did not believe themselves.

Keep in mind that the past no longer has any power over you. You can refuse to allow previous programming to rule your life any longer or to control your future. You are not doomed to a life of failure; you are totally in control. Giving up the past is the key to inner freedom. To begin the process of healing the past, you need to release it and forgive everyone you feel has hurt you. Leave the past behind and today will be the dawn of a new day.

The next step on the road to financial success is to change your negative attitudes regarding money. Anyone desiring financial independence can have it, but first he or she must leave behind their *scarcity consciousness* and develop a *prosperity consciousness*. People who are broke never seem to let themselves have money in their lives. Deep down they feel that they don't really deserve to get

6

ahead. This scarcity consciousness is related to the "I don't deserve good things" phenomenon, and low self-esteem is behind it. These people keep themselves poor. Even if they were to win the lottery, they would find a way to make all that money disappear as quickly as possible. The wealthy, on the other hand, have prosperity consciousness. They are always ready to accept the good that comes their way.

For generations we have been indoctrinated with the belief that money is somehow evil. If you want to attract money to you, you have to dispel the guilt that surrounds it. Money itself cannot be evil. It is only as good or as bad as the individual who possesses it.

Never feel bad about wanting a better life. We are not here just to survive and there is absolutely nothing wrong with wanting to be financially free. Just think of the good you could do with your wealth. You could make a big difference in the world and help a lot of people.

As you work to change your attitudes about money, be patient with yourself and others. Changing your negative habits will take time, but the good news is that you *can* change. Things are not hopeless. Remember, only you can alter your financial situation. The future starts today.

Change Your Attitude, Change Your Life

"Life is really very simple. What we give out, we get back."
— *Louise L. Hay*

Many people go through life hoping and dreaming that someday something wonderful will happen and make everything okay. In the meantime they work their 9-to-5 jobs, play the lottery, and/or go to the casinos, hopeful that this might be the day they hit the jackpot. Why are these people leaving their financial future up to chance?

"The reason is simple," says Chuck Chakrapani, author of *Financial Freedom on $5 a Day.* "We all want the good life. But we are not prepared to do what it takes to get there. We hope. We procrastinate and we hesitate."

The broke hope that someday a ton of money will fall into their laps, but they don't take responsibility for their lack of financial success. Here are just a few of the common reasons that they use:

- I'm not healthy enough.
- I'm not educated enough.
- I'm not intelligent or talented enough.
- I'm too young or too old.
- I'm not lucky enough/I was born under an unlucky star.

You get the point—excuses, excuses, and more excuses!

To Become Wealthy You Need to Bring Home a Large Paycheck: True or False?

"Being frugal is the cornerstone of wealth-building"
— Thomas Stanley & William Danko

The answer, of course, is *false*. If you believe you need a large paycheck to become wealthy, it is time to change that belief. Just because someone earns a lot of money does not necessarily mean that he or she will achieve financial success. It's not about how much money you make; it's about how much you keep. The person who has a regular habit of saving will always be financially ahead of the person who spends more than he or she makes, no matter how big their paychecks.

There are couples (I personally know some of them) who bring home a combined income of over $100,000 a year and have little to show for their work. Some of these high earners don't even have a pension plan in place. They live paycheck to paycheck.

In contrast, I also know people who bring in less than $60,000 a year and are wealthy. Many people with average incomes accumulate greater net worth than high earners. How is this possible? These disciplined people are less interested in luxurious living and more interested in saving. They have goals and dreams for their future,

9

such as accumulating a sizeable estate, and they work hard to make them a reality. They believe that an extravagant lifestyle is the privilege only of the super-rich, so they live modest lives below their means while investing their savings.

Don't get me wrong—these people live well. They are not sacrificing their happiness. They recognize that in order to reach their goals they need to stay on top of their finances. They know that the secret to wealth-building is self-control and patience—lots of patience—not necessarily high earnings. The belief that you have to make lots of money to be wealthy is a myth. Don't let it be an excuse for not achieving your dreams.

Why Are the Unsuccessful Irresponsible with Money?

Generally speaking, the broke are irresponsible with money. They think in all-or-nothing terms. If they can't put a good sum of money in savings, then it is not worth saving any at all. What they don't realize is that, if they don't save *any* of their money, they will not have any. Saving a little here and a little there really does add up.

"Money can't buy you happiness," they say. "It's only money. It's meant to be spent and you can't take it with you anyway." I can't tell you how many times I've heard this, and I believe that this attitude keeps them poor. However, I also feel that the broke don't really believe these statements. Just ask people you know who are in great financial difficulty if they are happy with their situation. Yet they continue to make poor financial choices. They just don't want to take the steps necessary to achieve financial satisfaction.

Yes, of course we should live life to the fullest each and every day. I don't endorse sacrificing present happiness to future financial freedom. We each have the right to treat ourselves to a nice holiday or a fancy dinner once in a while. Just like with everything in life, there needs to be balance. The secret to financial success is to learn how to manage your money well so you don't need to sacrifice happiness for financial freedom.

Are the Rich Really Different from the Poor?

Financial experts say that there is only a subtle difference between wealthy people and those who are broke. The difference is that the wealthy know that to achieve financial success, they must pay a price. That price is usually sacrifice and a lot of hard work, whether mental or physical.

It is not that the wealthy person is more intelligent or talented or better than the broke person. These characteristics are too often overrated, and a lack of talent or intelligence is frequently used as an excuse for failing to try. In fact, most of us are more creative than we think we are. We simply need to tap into our creativity and channel it outward.

The difference is simple: the rich have a winning attitude. That's all it takes, a subtle change in attitude that makes all the difference. How well you succeed and how much wealth you accumulate depends almost entirely on your willingness to work hard and persevere. The broke are defeated in life not because they lack ability, but because they lack the commitment to follow through.

It is not possible to achieve financial freedom if you are unwilling to change how you spend and save your money—your old habits will continue to keep you in the poorhouse. You need to overcome bad habits and develop a new attitude if you ever hope to become wealthy.

A Positive Attitude

A positive attitude towards life is essential to your success. Negative people focus on problems, find something to complain about, allow worry to rule them, and are cynical. Those with a positive attitude turn obstacles into opportunities, believe that things can get better, and focus on finding solutions.

So, how can we free ourselves from this negative attitude so that we can unblock our path to the happier, richer, fuller life we all deserve? You are already on the right path. The fact that you are reading this book proves that you want to live the financial dream. So, let's get started and work on changing some of these negative attitudes.

The Broke Are Always Broke

"Money is attracted to people who are strong and powerful, respectful of it, and open to receiving it."
— Suze Orman

The very attitudes and beliefs that you have about money can keep you broke. Here are some of those attitudes and beliefs of the unsuccessful and how you can change them:

1. The unsuccessful like to blame others for their situation. They may blame their parents, spouse, business partners, boss, bad luck, God—you name it. Please realize that blaming is a waste of time and that playing the role of victim will get you nowhere. In

13

particular, blaming others for your financial situation will only keep you poor. Dismiss the poor-me attitude that most unsuccessful people have. Instead, take responsibility for your situation and keep moving forward. None of us likes to make mistakes, and yet we all have and will continue to make them. Just learn from them.

2. Many unsuccessful people resent or envy those who are more financially successful than they are. But why? Successful people should be admired—you can bet that most of them have worked hard to get where they are. If you continue to resent the wealthy, you will stay poor. Instead, delight in the successes of others. The universe is abundant and there is plenty to go around. Try copying them. They can teach you a lot and their successes should be encouraging. If they can do it, so can you.

3. People who are broke may have an attitude of "I want it all and I want it now." They thrive on immediate gratification but don't want to do the work required for success. These wishful thinkers imagine that the only means of getting rich is winning the lottery or inheriting loads of money. Some even gamble what little money they do have in the hopes of getting rich. But just dreaming about getting rich is not going to

work. You must have a plan of action in place (more on this later).

4. Poor people believe that investing is just for the rich. They think that in order to invest money, they need to earn and have lots of money. This way of thinking will prevent them from ever starting to accumulate wealth. Realize that small, regular investments add up. Becoming wealthy is about taking small steps over a long period of time.

5. The broke tend to live beyond their means, spending their money mindlessly. The more they make, the more they spend. They tend to squander their money in an attempt to bring some fun into their lives. They reason that, since they will never have money for the "big stuff," they may as well indulge in the small stuff (magazines, movies, fancy coffees, eating out, clothes, etc.). However, by refraining from throwing away your money on inconsequential things, you can accumulate enough for the big things you really want.

6. With some knowledge and time, anyone can become wealthy. But patience is in short supply for the unsuccessful. Unfortunately, there are no shortcuts to becoming wealthy; nothing will drop into your lap. You must learn to be patient.

Now here are some of the attitudes and beliefs of the wealthy:

1. The wealthy never give up. They will do whatever it takes (as long as it is legal and moral, of course) to create success. If you take the time to study the wealthy, you will notice that they usually love what they do and are good at it.

2. The wealthy have a winning attitude. They don't allow past failures to stand in their way. Failure is not necessarily an obstacle, nor does it mean all is lost. They simply learn from their mistakes and move on.

3. The wealthy believe that hard work alone will not make you rich. Why? Because there are only so many hours in a day. Since the amount of time you can work is limited, the amount of money you can make is limited. So, they work to earn money for their investments, they buy assets that go up in value, and they limit their liabilities. They make their money work for them. Yes, the wealthy believe that working hard is important because that is how they are able to put aside enough money to invest.

4. Wealthy people manage their money well. They have good spending habits, living below their means. They are content to live with less until they have enough

16

money to have more. Then they will have the option to sit back and watch their money grow, working only when they choose to. That is what it means to be financially free.

5. The successful surround themselves with experts and those who have positive attitudes towards money. They believe that if you want to learn about making money, you need to spend time with people who have lots of it. They avoid complainers at all costs, believing that negative energy is infectious. They prefer to associate only with winners and will take advice only from people who are more successful than they are.

Ingredients to Financial Success

The following are the four ingredients to financial success:

1. Regular savings—By saving at least 10 percent of each paycheck, you will be well on your way to financial freedom.

2. Patience—When it comes to making money, time is the most important factor. The more time you give your money to grow, the more you make. This requires patience. If you lack the ability to delay gratification—

that is, if you want things *now*—you will find it very difficult to achieve your financial goals.

3. A plan of action—How are you going to achieve your goals of financial freedom? You must have a specific, step-by-step plan in place.

4. Investing—When you consistently invest the money you save, your money makes you more money.

We will talk more about these four ingredients to financial success in the rest of this book.

Chapter 2 * Spend Less, Save More

"If you want to get rich, focus on making, keeping and investing your money."
— T. Harv Eker

If you cannot control your spending, you will never get rich. Period. It doesn't take a brain surgeon to know that in order to save more money, you have to spend less. But an amazing number of people still don't understand this. Building wealth takes discipline and a few sacrifices along the way. What are you willing to sacrifice for a future of financial freedom? Are you willing to do whatever it takes? If your answer was "no" or even "maybe," then you are not ready. You might as well give this book to someone who is ready to benefit from it. But if you answered "yes" to this question, then you're well on your way. Let's learn how to manage our spending.

Keeping Track of Your Spending

Every day, people throw away their hard-earned cash on things they don't need. If you hope to ever build wealth, you must cut your cost of living and keep on top of your spending. Establish a new spending personality and make saving your first priority. Learn how to stretch each dollar as far as it can be stretched.

Do you know where your money goes? How much of it you are spending on things you don't need? This part of the book will help you answer these questions.

For the next couple of weeks, keep track of all your spending. Carry a small notebook and a pen wherever you go. Write down every single purchase you make, no matter how small. Yes, even the 45-cent stamp and your morning cup of coffee. It doesn't matter how you pay for your purchases—with cash, debit card, or credit card. Record every cent. Your spending journal should look something like this:

My Spending Journal

Today's Date: Monday, June 22, 2007

Amount	Description
$ 3.99	Coffee and muffin
$ 6.25	Salad and Diet Coke for lunch
$ 3.75	Tall non-fat latte (mid-afternoon snack)
$ 30.00	Gas
$ 26.75	Groceries
$ 55.48	Phone bill
$ 126.22	Total

Today's Date: Tuesday, June 23, 2007

Amount	Description
$ 4.25	Coffee and bagel
$ 5.25	Magazine
$ 1.50	Parking meter
$ 15.00	Dry cleaning
$ 30.00	Birthday gift for a friend
$ 56.00	Total

You get the point. Do this every day for two weeks or longer. At the end of each day, total your expenses. At the end of the two weeks, evaluate your spending habits. Now ask yourself, "Have I spent more in two weeks than I have made?" Just knowing where your money is going can help you spend less of it.

Determining Your Expenses

Okay, now that you know how much you're spending, it's time to adjust your spending habits. Let's start by determining your essential and non-essential expenses.

Essential Expenses

Essential expenses are those that you must pay regularly: weekly, monthly, or annually. They can be broken into two types: fixed and variable. *Fixed essential expenses* are the same every month. They include your rent or mortgage payment, car payment, property taxes, insurance, and so on. *Variable essential expenses* vary from month to month. They include groceries, utilities, child-related expenses (such as sitters, diapers, and formula), and so on.

Non-Essential Expenses

Non-essential expenses (also called *discretionary expenses*) are for things that you want rather than need. Some examples of non-essential expenses are

- nonessential utilities: cable, satellite, internet access, and cell phone

- magazines and newspaper subscriptions
- restaurant meals and expensive convenience foods
- movies
- designer clothes and shoes
- vacations

  and so on.

Now that you know where your money is going and have learned the difference between essential and non-essential expenses, look at your spending journal and determine how much of your money is spent on non-essentials. Now comes the hard part—it is time to find ways to reduce your expenses.

The secret to becoming money smart is to look for ways to reduce your expenses without lowering the quality of your life. Which non-essential expenses can you do without? And are there ways in which you can reduce your essential expenses? It helps if you don't think of good money management as a sacrifice. You don't have to lower your standard of living or deprive yourself. In fact, reducing your expenses may very well give you a feeling of empowerment and improve the quality of your life.

Be kind to yourself. Realize that good habits take time to cultivate and your spending habits aren't going to change overnight. But if you truly want to change, in time you will pick up better spending habits. Keep your eyes on the prize, whatever that prize may be for you. Believe in yourself and your ability to control your own destiny.

Trimming Expenses

In a 2001 survey of household spending, Statistics Canada found that the average Canadian family spent $57,730 that year.

You don't have to spend a small fortune to have a good quality of life. For example, instead of always buying entertainment, try using your creative skills. It is surprising how a dollar here and a dollar there add up to big savings.

Next time you have the urge to splurge, stop and think. Think of all the times you've bought things on a whim. Most impulse spending is a waste of money. Just walk around your house and look at all your impulse purchases (cosmetics, shoes, clothes, CD's, kitchen gadgets, etc., etc., etc.). How many of them do you use? How many of them could you have done without? Think of all the money you could save if you cut down on impulse spending.

An important part of controlling your impulse spending is to recognize any triggers, such as depression, competition, or a desire to impress, that drive you to buy things. Then, instead of buying things on a whim, learn to make informed purchases based on your financial goals. This certainly doesn't mean that you can never treat yourself, but plan your treat carefully by giving yourself a set amount to spend.

Forgoing something now will pay off down the road. Focus on your dream of becoming financially free and work hard to make it happen. Your dreams are worth a little forethought and sacrifice, don't you agree?

20 Money-Saving Tips

Here is a list of 20 ways to save or make some money:

1. Your car can be your biggest expense. Keeping it maintained properly can save you money. Always check the warranty before paying for any repairs; it may cover some expenses. If the cost of a repair sounds unreasonable, get a second opinion. If you're thinking of buying a brand new car, think again. A two- to four-year-old car in good condition will cost less to purchase and insure and will depreciate more slowly than a new car.

2. If you don't use your gym membership (or if you don't go often enough to get your money's worth), cancel it. There are many fun ways to exercise for free or for a very low cost, such as walking on a nature trail,

jogging in a park, rollerblading, biking, dancing, swimming, and playing tennis.

3. If you can, book trips at the last minute. Most travel agencies offer big discounts at the last minute in order to fill spaces. Or forgo your expensive yearly vacation this year. Go camping, rent a cottage near a lake, or take a short trip closer to home.

4. Look for bargains. When shopping for groceries, buy no-name or store brands instead of more costly name brands. Stock up on sale items, but buy only those that you use. Shop at discount or warehouse stores, where you can often buy the same items for less.

5. Shop less. Every time you go to the store, you buy more than you intended. By limiting shopping trips, you avoid costly impulse purchases. Write a list and stick to it.

6. Eat more meals at home. Restaurant food is not only expensive, it is also high in calories and saturated fat. For a special treat, pack a picnic basket, head to the beach or park, and watch the sunset.

7. Instead of buying expensive bottled water, use a water filtration system.

8. Break the junk food habit and you could save $40 to $50 a week. That adds up to over $2,000 a year.

9. Instead of buying lunch every day, take your lunch to work. A deli sandwich at $5 a day can easily add up to $1,000 a year. As a bonus, you'll probably eat healthier.

10. Do you know how much your coffee habit is costing you? Spending $4 a day on coffee adds up to over $1,400 a year. Cut your habit by half and save a lot of money.

11. Rent a video instead of going to the movies. It is cheaper and a lot more cozy and private. Many libraries have a good selection of movies that you can borrow for free. Don't forget the popcorn!

12. If you smoke, quit! Your habit is costing you a small fortune—$1,500 a year or more—not to mention what it is doing to your health.

13. Organize a garage sale. This is a good way to clear out clutter as well as make some extra cash. You'll save even more if you can clear out an expensive storage unit.

14. If you are a reader like me and own a lot of books, sell those you no longer want to used bookstores.

15. Sell your gently used clothing, shoes, and accessories to consignment stores. This is another good way to clear some clutter in your house and make some extra cash.

16. Return your pop, beer, and juice cans to get the deposit back. Every little bit counts.

17. Every night put the small change from your pockets or purse into a jar. This could add up to over $1,000 a year.

18. Seek ways to earn additional income. You can do this by working overtime or by taking a temporary job.

19. Start a small home business that you can work at in the evenings and on weekends. Make sure it is something you enjoy doing.

20. If you have an extra room in your house, rent it to a foreign student for an extra $600 to $750 a month. There are agencies that can help you with this and they take their fee from the students. People who have two or three spare rooms can make big bucks doing this.

Hidden Expenses

By recognizing and avoiding hidden expenses, you can trim your spending. Some hidden expenses are

- bank and ATM fees
- credit card fees
- annual fees
- high interest charges
- below-minimum-balance fees

- late-payment penalties
- per-use fees

Many people don't have a clue as to what kind of hidden fees they are paying or how much it's costing them. It's time to get informed. Read all the information you receive from banks, credit card companies, and other financial institutions, and don't hesitate to ask questions about the fees you are paying and how you can lower or eliminate them altogether. Remember that every dollar you spend on hidden expenses is a dollar you don't have to put towards your financial dream.

So, what are you going to do with all the extra money you've saved by reducing your expenses? It should go toward two things:

1. paying down your debts
2. contributing to your savings plan.

The work you've done is starting to pay off. By watching your spending, you get to enjoy seeing your debts disappear and your savings grow as you get closer to achieving your financial goals.

Debt Control

"If you have difficulty sustaining a lifestyle or position, you have trapped yourself."
— Stuart Wilde

The next step towards your goal of financial freedom is to pay off your debts. Debts are the most serious obstacle to achieving financial success, so getting out of debt should be a top priority. Debts are stressful—no doubt about it. Lift this burden.

Concentrate on one debt at a time. Pay off your higher interest bill first and then move on to the next. Don't fool yourself—it will take discipline and sacrifice. But by changing your spending habits and establishing a new spending personality, you will have more money available to put towards your debts. The trick to paying them off as quickly as possible is to spend less and pay more against your bills.

It is especially important that you take control of your credit cards. The more you use them, the more the credit card company will try to entice you by raising your available credit. This can be a problem for people who have trouble managing credit. If you can't use credit cards responsibly, get rid of them. You will be doing yourself a big favor. Get in the habit of paying for your purchases in cash, or, if you can't do this, don't make the purchase. If you have to charge it, you probably can't afford it.

If you must, keep just one card for emergencies only. I suggest you protect yourself from yourself by having the credit card company lower your available credit to $1,000 or even $500. Do your best to pay the bill off in full and on time every month to avoid unnecessary interest payments and costly late fees. When you carry a balance, you are giving your money away to the credit card company.

Avoid department store credit cards at all costs. They usually have a higher interest rate than bank credit cards.

If you are in serious debt trouble I suggest you get help from a credit counseling service. These professionals can help you regain control of your finances and give you a fresh start.

Saving for a Rainy Day

Before you start saving for investment purposes, you should build an emergency fund in case of a financial blow like the loss of a job or an unexpected illness. Save as much as possible until you have put aside four to six months of living expenses in a high-interest savings account. This money should be used only in an emergency. No exceptions! And no, a vacation is not an emergency.

Investing in Your Future

Now that you've cut down on your spending, eliminated your debts, and established an emergency fund, it's time to come up with the money you will need to start investing. As your financial situation improves, you can increase the amount you save. The faster your investment savings grow, the more quickly you can invest them, and the faster your money will make more money. Remember that you are saving in order to be in a position to finance your dreams, and to do so you must stay the course.

First, decide how much you can comfortably put into your savings account each month. This is the money you will use to make your financial dreams a reality. You should aim to save at least 10 percent of your gross income each month, no matter how much you earn. This one step will dramatically increase your chances of financial security. If you can, put aside a little more, but remember that something is always better than nothing.

Then set up a high-interest savings account for your investment money and talk to your bank clerk about making an automatic monthly transfer from your checking account to this account. This bill—to yourself—will be the first one you pay every month. Your investment account should not be used for anything other than investing and saving for your retirement. Add to this account whenever you can.

When you have accumulated enough funds, start investing your money. You may want to start a small business, or buy some real estate that will generate rental income, or invest in the stock market. Enlist the help of a qualified financial planner if you don't feel you can do it on your own.

Investing for the Long Term

Income comes in two forms: working income and passive income. Generally speaking, working income is the money you earn from your work (your day job). And passive income is money that is working for you (money earned through investments). Your goal to becoming financially free is to earn more passive income. This is where investing comes in.

Investing—we all say we are going to do it someday, right? But it's easier said than done. The main idea behind investing is to use an amount of money to make a larger amount of money. When you put money in an interest-bearing savings account, your financial institution pays interest into your account. If you don't touch the interest, but instead allow it to be added to your lump sum, then you start to earn interest on the interest. This is the magic of compound interest, a powerful tool that can provide considerable wealth.

People who are successful at investing are the ones who don't view it as a get-rich-quick scheme. Investing requires a bit of knowledge and a lot of patience. There are many investment strategies available today, but one that has helped a lot of people become wealthy is the buying and holding of stocks and mutual funds for a long period of time. You would be amazed at how hard a relatively small amount of money can work for you if you just leave it alone.

Of course, the earlier you start saving, the more you make from compound interest. Let me give you an example. Let's say you invest $5,000 at age 25 at a 10 percent annual rate of return, which is the average the stock market has returned for many years. Assume that the interest is compounded monthly and you leave it alone until you retire. By age 50 you will have well over $98,000, and by age 65 you will have over $593,000. Not bad, right?

Here are a few more examples: Invest $1,000 at an annual growth rate of 10 percent for 20 years, and your money will grow to $6,727. Invest $20,000 at an annual growth rate of 10 percent for 20 years, and its value will grow to $134,550. You get the idea. The longer you leave your money, the more powerful the compound interest.

Rich people buy luxuries last, while the poor and middle class tend to buy luxuries first.

— *Robert T. Kiyosaki*, Rich Dad, Poor Dad

Chapter 3 * Live the Life You Deserve

Money is one of the most important subjects of your entire life. Some of life's greatest enjoyments and most of life's greatest disappointments stem from your decisions about money. Whether you experience great peace of mind or constant anxiety will depend on getting your finances under control.

— Robert G Allen

A well-thought-out financial strategy can help you achieve your goals of saving for retirement, sending your kids to college, buying your dream home, or whatever they might be. But how do you get started? Start by

1. setting financial goals
2. determining how much you will need to save for your goals
3. selecting an investment strategy.

Once you are totally committed to becoming wealthy and you are willing to hold nothing back, you will be amazed at how quickly things start to fall into place. The universe will support your efforts and great things will start to happen in your life.

What are you waiting for? Remember that the sooner you start to use your creativity, the quicker you will succeed. Follow sound advice, don't be afraid to take a chance, and pursue your hunches.

Start making your financial dream a reality by following these three simple steps: goal setting, determining how much you need to save, and selecting an investment strategy.

Goal Setting

Setting goals is the foundation to financial success. It's quite difficult to get what you want if you don't know what it is. Like a road map, a plan tells you where you are and where you want to be. Once you know what you want and need, you can start thinking about how you will get it.

Take some time to think about how you plan to become financially free. Write down what you are trying to do and when you would like to achieve it (I have included pages in the back of this booklet for this purpose). Be specific.

Next, ask yourself, "What's stopping me?" Write down any obstacles in your way. Then figure out how you are going to overcome each of them. Read what you have written from time to time and make any necessary changes.

Now that you know what your goals are, you have to act on them by taking educated, calculated risks. You can read all the books and attend all the financial seminars you want, but unless you implement what you learn, nothing will change in your life. No more hoping and dreaming—it's time to take action. Winning starts with beginning, so take that all-important first step.

Determining How Much You Need to Save

How much will you need to start saving for your goals? Well, that depends on what they are. Let's say your first goal (after paying of all your debts) is to buy a house. Break out the calculator and do the math. Figure out the size of down payment you need and how much a mortgage will cost you (I will talk more about real-estate investing later).

Selecting an Investment Strategy

Investing the money you save from your day job is probably the most powerful and successful way there is to make money. There are several places to invest your money, including a business, real estate, and the stock market. Let's take a brief look at each of these.

Owning Your Own Business

Owning a business is a dream for many people. But before you give up the security of your job, be aware of the pitfalls. Every year, several hundred thousand new enterprises are started and, regrettably, almost as many close shop, usually within the first five years. Having said that, if owning your own business is your dream and if you are determined, can provide a product or service that is wanted or needed by others, and are willing to work hard at it, you can succeed.

The most common reasons for business failure are managerial incompetence and lack of experience. Before investing in your own business, do your homework. Develop the knowledge you will need, not only in your area of interest, but also in running and managing a company.

Remember, anyone can start a business. The trick is to make a success of it. People who run truly profitable businesses are those who do the things they enjoy the most. Profits, ambitions, and lifestyles go hand in hand.

Good luck!

The Real-Estate Market

Most of us dream of owning our own home. There is really nothing quite like the security and pride that it brings. If you don't own your own home, I would highly recommend that you consider making this one of your financial goals. You can usually get a mortgage for a house or an apartment for the same amount of money you spend on rent. It makes more sense to put that money towards something of your own, right?

You may be wondering how you could ever come up with 20 to 25 percent of the purchase price for a down payment. For many first-time homebuyers, this seems like an impossible dream. But it is usually not the case that you need a huge down payment. There are programs that allow first-time homebuyers to finance as much as 95 percent of the price of the property, if they have a solid credit history and income.

Remember that nothing is impossible if you want it badly enough. Start by talking with a mortgage broker or a mortgage expert at your bank and by making a priority of saving for a down payment.

Financing Your Property

Talbot Stevens, author of *Financial Freedom without Sacrifice* says, "The right way to look at a mortgage is as a leveraged, forced savings plan into what has historically been one of the best investments—real estate." A mortgage forces you to save for your future because if you don't make your payments, you will lose your home. A pretty good incentive, don't you think?

When buying a home, it is important that you don't overextend yourself by going beyond your means. It is always wise to start small. You don't have to impress anyone—you just want to get into the market. When your property's value rises, you can sell it in order to buy something bigger and better. As a general rule, your mortgage should be no more than 25 to 30 percent of your yearly income. Of course, that's assuming you don't have a lot of other debt. Again, talk to a mortgage expert at your bank; he or she will help you determine how much you can afford.

You must be smart about how you finance your new home or you might waste a fortune. There are many types of mortgages, each with advantages and disadvantages, so it pays to do your research and to shop around for the best rate. Even a one-percent difference can add up to a lot of money over the term of your mortgage.

Your goal should be to pay down your mortgage debt as quickly as possible so that you don't spend a fortune on interest. Talk to your mortgage broker or bank manager about setting up a biweekly payment plan. By making a payment every two weeks instead of once a month, you end up making one extra month's payment each year, which means you will pay off your mortgage early and save thousands of dollars in interest—a simple plan that really works.

You can get mortgage information at your bank or credit union or from a mortgage broker. These experts can explain the various types of available mortgages. In addition, there are many great books on how to finance your first home. I recommend that you read a few of them so that you can make intelligent choices with your money.

Real-Estate Investing

If building wealth is your goal, then buying real estate is the way to go. Purchasing an investment property is one of smartest long-term financial decisions you'll ever make. My husband and I have been real-estate investors for over two decades now and it has worked out well for us. We encourage our children to do the same. Many people become rich just by investing in real estate.

When investing in real estate, you must think long term. This type of asset will appreciate over time, but you have to be prepared to stick with it. There are no guarantees that your property will rise in value every

43

single year, but many experts believe that the only way you can lose in real-estate investments is if you're forced to sell in a down market. Rent your property out so that someone else is paying your mortgage, hold onto it until it goes up in value, and then sell it for a profit. You can add value to your rental property by renovating; even minor renovations such as a new floor or fresh paint will increase its value.

One word of caution: It is very important that you buy only what you can afford now; never overextend your finances. Just as with any other investment, it is vital that you educate yourself and start small until you develop the skills and knowledge necessary for taking bigger risks.

While many people make plenty of money by flipping properties, investing in real estate is not for everyone. I do not advise it for the novice investor or for those with poor timing or judgment. Buying and selling properties is a business that takes a lot of time, knowledge, and patience, as well as the right temperament. If you believe you have what it takes, make sure you understand the risks involved.

Investing in the Stock Market

Financial experts believe that one of the closest things to a worry-free wealth-building strategy is to invest, long term, in the stock market. However, if you're thinking short term, this type of investing is not for you. Stock market investments may lose value at times, but over the long term these investments provide good returns.

Once you have your nest egg, you can start to build an investment portfolio you are comfortable with and understand. And you don't need a fortune to get started. A good place to begin is with mutual funds.

Although many people find investing in the stock market and mutual funds intimidating, it need not be. With the help of a qualified financial expert you should be able to find a fund that is right for you. Educate yourself and look for an honest, dependable financial planner with whom you feel comfortable. Get referrals from friends and family who are doing well with their investments. And remember, always stay within your comfort zone.

Before you speak, listen. Before you write, think. Before you spend earn. Before you invest, investigate. Before you criticize, wait. Before you pray, forgive. Before you quit, try. Before you retire, save. Before you die, give.

— *William A. Ward*

Chapter 4 * On a Personal Note

Financial education needs to become a part of our national curriculum and scoring systems so that it's not just the rich kids that learn about money... it's all of us.
— *David Bach*

In this final chapter I am going to get a little personal. I will briefly touch on the following subjects:

- the importance of protecting your dependents
- why you should teach your children about money
- what to do if you are in a relationship with a big spender
- why taking care of your health is important, and last but not least
- nurturing your personal relationships.

Now let's get started.

Protecting Your Dependents

Nothing is more important than the security of your loved ones. If you have dependents—children or other relatives who depend on you financially—you must protect them. Buy life and health insurance and have an up-to-date will in place.

Purchase adequate health insurance to provide for you and your dependents in the event that you are no longer able to earn an income. Life insurance will financially protect your dependents if you pass away. By buying insurance, you can help to ensure that your family will be able to maintain a reasonable standard of living if you are not able to work or if something unexpected happens to you. Consult with a financial advisor who is licensed to sell insurance.

If you pass away without a will, it falls to the government to figure out what should be done with your estate. Do you really want the government to decide how your assets will be divided up?

Protect what's yours and take the necessary steps so that if you are no longer able to work or if you pass away your family doesn't suffer unfortunate financial ramifications.

Raising Money-Smart Kids

Teaching your children about money is one of the greatest gifts you can give them. But, regrettably, it is too often neglected. Think for a moment about how your own life might have been different if your parents taught you the importance of being responsible with your money. Although there are no guarantees in life, if your children have a sound financial education they are less likely to have financial problems.

Now more than ever before parents need to give their children the tools to manage their money. It is our responsibility to raise financially literate kids. Sending our children out into the world without these necessary money skills can have a devastating effect on their financial future. Poor money skills can lead to a life of stressful money struggles.

When you give money to your kids, do it in a way that teaches them about finance and money management. Kids who are given whatever their little hearts desire and grow up watching parents indulge themselves do not learn the value of money. Of course we want to make things easier for our kids than we had it, but no one wants to raise a greedy, lazy, or spoiled child. The fact remains that giving them everything they want on a silver platter teaches only poor financial responsibility. If we as

49

parents set a good example and guide our children in responsible money management, we can stop the cycle of financial illiteracy.

You might be wondering how you can educate your children about money when you have only a basic understanding of financial matters yourself. Please, don't let your lack of money skills stop you from educating your children. If you don't do it, no one else will. This stuff is not always taught in school, although I believe it should be.

Start by teaching your children that money should be used respectfully and talk to them about how it can help them lead a better life. Always lead by example because your children learn more from what you do than from what you say. Educate yourself so that you can in turn teach your children.

The overall idea is not difficult. Spend less than you have. Save the difference. Watch it grow. Easy, right? Kids (as well as some adults) must learn that they can't escape the first law of financial discretion: spend less than you earn!

There are some wonderful books on this subject. I highly recommend *Allowances Dollars and Sense: A Proven System for Teaching Your Kids about Money* by Canadian author Paul W. Lermitte. Lermitte presents a step-by-step system for teaching children about money based on giving them a regular allowance. By teaching your kids lessons in saving, spending, and giving to charities of their choice, you will raise financially independent and responsible adults.

Are You in a Relationship with a Spender?

Spenders are usually compulsive shoppers who feel the urge to spend and often buy on impulse things they can't really afford or don't even need. Most spenders are live-for-today type people. Money seems to burn a hole in their pockets. Living with a spender can be challenging, to say the least.

Money is a common source of conflict among couples and is to blame for many fights and separations. Please don't let this happen to you. If you are married or in a committed relationship with a spender or someone who is just plain irresponsible with money, don't despair. The good new is that most marital money problems are fixable with enough patience and time. Few couples share exactly the same attitudes and habits concerning money. The successful ones are those who figure out how to deal with this fact and come up with a solution together.

The first step in resolving financial disagreements is to help your spouse understand that if you are both to live a life free of worry about money, you will need to work together and to set goals. If you work as a team, your potential for financial success is enormous. Use the skills you have learned in this and other books to help your partner understand how money works and how he or she too can become more prosperity minded.

Keep in mind that the spender lives for the moment and usually doesn't think twice about unnecessary spending, like buying lunch or specialty coffee for an afternoon pick-me-up five days a week. Help your loved one understand just how much these little indulgences cost over time. For example, spending $15.00 a day on lunch and coffee five days a week adds up to $3,900.00 a year. This money could be put aside for your financial goals or even for a relaxing vacation to Mexico or Hawaii. Remind your spouse that sometimes you have to give up something to gain something even better. Be patient and caring—changing long-standing habits takes time, but your spouse is likely to come around. If your partner has a more serious problem, such as gambling, you both need to seek professional help.

In the meantime you must take control of most of the finances. It might help to set up a joint account into which both your paychecks are deposited. Then make arrangements with your bank to automatically transfer a set amount every week into separate checking accounts. This is your spending money for the week, to do with as you please. You might also consider making an agreement that neither of you is to spend over $100 without consulting the other.

Health Is Wealth

Many people sacrifice their health in the name of success. They expose themselves to a lot of stress; live on fast food, too much alcohol, and coffee; smoke; don't get enough sleep; and don't exercise, all to make more money.

Good health is the foundation for a more abundant and fulfilling life. You cannot enjoy your wealth without you health. Illness will stop you in your tracks and keep you from progressing with your financial plan. We all know this, yet our lives are so fast paced and full of pressure that it is sometimes difficult to find the time to take care of ourselves. Remember that on your deathbed, you're not likely to wish that you had worked more.

Make an effort to make wiser dietary and lifestyle choices in order to reduce your risk of disease. A healthy diet consists of whole-grain foods, eggs, chicken, fish, vegetables (especially the dark leafy variety), fruit, and legumes (beans). Limit alcohol, coffee, and soda, and don't smoke. Replace margarine with olive oil and small amounts of butter, and limit red meat and simple carbohydrates (white flour, white sugar, and their products, including junk foods). Drink plenty of water and get plenty of fresh air and exercise. A healthy lifestyle will also help keep you within a healthy weight range, and you will find that your mind is clearer and your day much more productive.

Start making positive changes in your life now, not after the fact. When we possess good health, we already have wealth, so treasure it and preserve it. Remember, you are your most valuable asset.

Nurture Your Personal Relationships

Ask yourself whether you are willing to sacrifice your important personal relationships in the name of success. I hope you answered "no"! Loving, nurturing relationships are one of life's greatest pleasures and they account for a huge part of our overall happiness.

A healthy relationship with your spouse or significant other is very important not only to your happiness, but also to your financial future. Studies show that happily married people live longer, are healthier, earn (and accumulate) more money, and feel more fulfilled in their lives than do single or divorced people. Remember also that divorce is the largest financial litigation in the nation. Don't let this happen to you.

So, if you long for a deeply fulfilled life, nurture your personal relationships every day. Keep in mind that two is always more powerful than one; stick together, think as a couple, and include each other in all decision making. And don't buy into the myth that you have to forgo your happiness to achieve success.

Enjoy life, enjoy each other, and remember that we are not here just to accomplish goals.

Have some fun!

Empty pockets never held anyone back. Only empty heads and empty hearts can do that.

— *Norman Vincent Peale*

A Final Note

Thank you for reading *The Little Gold Book of Money and Happiness*. While the book is done, your journey to financial fulfillment has just begun—you have much more work to do. I encourage you to continue to educate yourself about money matters. I have recommended below some of my favorite personal finance books. I believe you will find them very useful and enjoyable.

Before I go, I would like to leave you with a quote from Robert Kiyosaki, author of *Rich Dad, Poor Dad*, who sums it all up beautifully.

With each dollar bill that enters your hand, you and only you have the power to determine your destiny. Spend it foolishly, you choose to be poor. Spend it on liabilities, you join the middle class. Invest it in your mind and learn how to acquire assets and you will be choosing wealth as your goal and your future. The choice is yours and only yours.

I wish you perfect health, wealth, and much happiness!

Joanne B. Parrotta

57

He who loses money, loses much; He who loses a friend loses much more; He who loses faith, loses all.

— *Eleanor Roosevelt*

My Top Picks for Personal Finance Books

Rich Dad, Poor Dad: What the Rich Teach Their Kids about Money That the Poor and Middle Class Do Not! by Robert T. Kiyosaki with Sharon L. Lechter. Warner Books, 1998.

The Automatic Millionaire: A Powerful One-Step Plan to Live and Finish Rich by David Bach. Doubleday Canada, 2003.

Secrets of the Millionaire Mind: Mastering the Inner Game of Wealth by T. Harv Eker. HarperCollins, 2005.

Financial Freedom without Sacrifice by Talbot Stevens. Financial Success Strategies, 1993.

Financial Freedom on $5 a Day by Chuck Chakrapani. Self-Counsel Press, 1994.

The 9 Steps to Financial Freedom: Practical and Spiritual Steps So You Can Stop Worrying by Suze Orman. Crown Publishers, 1997.

The Trick to Money Is Having Some! by Stuart Wilde. Hay House, 1989.

Mind Power into the 21st Century by John Kehoe. Zoetic Inc., 1997.

Allowances Dollars and Sense: A Proven System for Teaching Your Kids about Money by Paul Lermitte. McGraw-Hill, 1999.

The Millionaire Next Door: The Surprising Secrets of America's Wealthy by Thomas J. Stanley and William D. Danko. Simon and Schuster, 2000.

The Courage to Be Rich: Creating a Life of Material and Spiritual Abundance by Suze Orman. Riverhead, 2001.

Average Family's Guide to Financial Freedom: How You Can Save a Small Fortune on a Modest Income by Bill Toohey and Mary Toohey. John Wiley and Sons Canada, 2000.

Your Money or Your Life: Transforming Your Relationship with Money and Achieving Financial Independence by Joe Dominguez and Vicki Robin. Penguin, 1999.

Other Books by Joanne B. Parrotta

CR

A Matter of Destiny

How to Find and Marry Your Soulmate—A Beginner's Guide
(BookSurge Publishing, 2006)

Just imagine finally being with your true love—that wonderful feeling of completeness, knowing that you've found your meant-to-be love and that there is no one else in the world you would rather be with.

Sound impossible? I would like to introduce you to *A Matter of Destiny: How to Find and Marry Your Soulmate—A Beginner's Guide*.

A Matter of Destiny is for those who have experienced disappointment in love and wondered if they will ever find happiness in a relationship. Aimed at the single person looking for more than just a casual date or another dead-end relationship, it is for those who crave that special soulful connection that only soulmates naturally share.

For more visit: *http://www.amatterofdestiny.com.*

The Promiscuous Woman:

Modern Attitudes about Love **and Sex**

(WiseAdviceBooks, 2007)

Promiscuity is a serious problem in North America. We live in a society saturated with pornography, where many fear commitment, where having sex by the third date is the norm and where being promiscuous in portrayed as something to be proud of. This hooking-up culture, created perhaps by the sex-crazed media and the sexual revolution of the mid-to late-1960s, can have many psychological and emotional consequences.

If you are a promiscuous single woman or know someone who is, then you won't want to pass up on this thought provoking little book, visit **www.wiseadvicebooks.com** or **www.lulu.com** for more information and to order.

More Books from the *WiseAdviceBooks Series*

Coming Soon!

Notes

_____

_____

_____

_____

_____

_____

_____

_____

_____

_____

_____

If a person gets his attitude toward money straight, it will help straighten out most every other area in his life.

— *Billy Graham*

A Great Gift!

We hope you have enjoyed reading *The Little Gold Book of Money and Happiness*. Could someone you know benefit from reading it as well? It is the perfect gift for someone wanting a better life.

For instructions on how you can order more books visit the publisher's website
http://www.lulu.com/content/894750.

To contact the author and learn more about her works visit:
www.amatterofdestiny.com and www.wiseadvicebooks.com.

www.ingramcontent.com/pod-product-compliance
Lightning Source LLC
Chambersburg PA
CBHW021902170526
45157CB00005B/1924